Praise for Jeff Hardin

" '...So often anything returned to is an absence weighed / against a self the self no longer is nor cares to be. / A sparrow, steering skyward, stalls the present tense.' In these quiet descriptive/meditative poems, Jeff Hardin questions experience: what is a voice, what are words, what is a day? He offers readers a wealth of opportunities to meander in the company of tutelary spirits—birds, rivers, trees, Dickinson, Issa, Stafford, and Bach, among others—seeking ever deeper wonder, 'to touch existence on the face' rather than achieve resolution. This is a book of refreshment for a turbulent time."
– Claire Bateman, author of *Wonders of the Invisible World*

"The poems in Jeff Hardin's *Coming into an Inheritance*, skyscrapers tethered by trapeze, wheel within their structural constraints freely and with fervor. This book—this poet—is indispensable, as these quasi-sonnets splinter our mutual malaise into ecstatic beauty. Hardin surveys out his window, seeks 'a way to stand inside a silence that erases me.' Silence, for this poet, is our holy grail; utterance, then, is what dams the cup. These flawless poems seek not answers but 'a word, then quiet, then what's after that.' "
– Gary McDowell, author of *Aflame*

"Jeff Hardin's *Coming into an Inheritance* offers a vision of poetry so filled with warmth, so generous in spirit, that to read the book is to experience the waters where Robert Frost promises we may 'drink and be whole again beyond confusion.' Hardin's poems embrace paradox, perplexity, and fulfillment as equal stations on the journey—in one poem, the speaker says, 'I love a song whose only word, repeated, is 'rejoice.'/All my favorite words are variations on this theme.' There is also a special pleasure, a sense of accumulation, in seeing a poet find a form that seems the perfect container for their meanings as Hardin has done with his tercet-lined poems of five stanzas each. Galway Kinnell said that 'The secret title of every good poem could be 'Tenderness,' and Jeff Hardin gives us a full-hearted confirmation of this sentiment in *Coming into an Inheritance*."
– Jesse Graves, author of *Merciful Days* and *Tennessee Landscape with Blighted Pine*

COMING INTO AN
INHERITANCE

JEFF HARDIN

Publisher's Cataloguing-in-Publication Data

Hardin, Jeff
       Coming into an inheritance / written by Jeff Hardin
       ISBN: 978-1-953932-42-6

1. Poetry: General 2. Poetry: American – General 3. Poetry: Southern
Gothic
I. Title II. Author

Library of Congress Control Number: 2025951381

For Storie and Eli

Table of Contents

Assembling Many Voices

Another Language

Toward an Answering Day

Coming into an Inheritance

Assembling Many Voices

Taking on Other Voices

That some will take on voices, imagining lives
not their own, in times they never knew, must
mean a tenderness still moves within the world.

Trout-streams ride twists and turns, then circle
back, a logic whose biting cold a man can stand in
far from agendas, pogroms, polemics, affairs of state.

What is a day anyway? I like the case Issa makes
describing himself as *so-so*. A cardinal hopping
higher up the limbs suggests I'm less than that.

Let's get down in the weeds where crickets live.
Let's call it delight we even exist. Let's let the weight
of who we think we are be caught up and cleansed.

This reach for meaning means the mind is never
satisfied, or new proofs will soon appear, or there's
so much manifest a single mind cannot keep up.

Following Minnows Upstream

I go back through years, along trails and then up
hillsides, down through hollows, trying to find
that place I first knelt and knew I was being born.

Anyone who knows me understands I'm a hermit
found sometimes wandering in the marketplace.
Or maybe an ancestor is looking through my eyes?

So many decrees from my culture I choose to ignore.
One explanation I'll offer, if asked, is how often,
with great focus, I've followed a minnow upstream.

Lately—though I'm content to discover otherwise—
I've determined a little wandering might be necessary
to get to a place beyond the place I think I'm going.

Having been witness to moonlight bathing stones,
I plead each moment's passing is a benediction,
though our time together is never concluded.

Jeff Hardin

Morning Light Along Sage Grass

Where is the poem where we hold out our hands,
Van Goghs wandering an empty canvas, searching
for a landscape to rival the hues of our dreams?

Birdsong, thistlesong, cool wind against sweatsong—
this world is a wound and a wish, an excess, a lack,
three dropped plums sating roots near the fencerow.

I once knew my name but then gave it away. Now
I'm morning light rising up the length of sage grass,
reaching heavenward and swaying slightly east.

My enemies—such a long line of disbelievers.
I imagine them bent to cup water from a spring,
weeping for themselves but somehow not knowing.

One day grief will be all that I am. I'll lie down
among ferns and be no one. My eyes will be
pocks of rain on dust, then nothing, then gone.

I Remain Unconvinced

Friends listening in may find me speaking to the void,
a daily habit, for how else know the debt I owe for
having lived? Such an intoxicant, a thousand windows!

I'm fond of saying these words I seek are already
posthumous. You on your side, me on mine, but perhaps
we're blind and crawl toward touching some middle place.

I remain unconvinced that moonlight isn't fragrant.
I remain unconvinced that Dickinson's letters weren't
meant for me, for now and then I certainly receive them.

That first poet who equated blood with ink forgot that
one is slow to dry and the other quick to spread beyond
its boundaries. And both stain, both blossom, both redeem.

Some say we are exiles, wandering toward a place remote
and possibly non-existent, but I say there's a word or two
we've found, born from between us, and we are not empty.

Jeff Hardin

Studying the Sages

All these years I've studied how sages found
their joy. Now look at me—I'm destitute. They
gave me to thirst, which has led me to grace.

When I was eight, I used to lay my head on
moss and stare up through mimosa limbs. No
wonder my mind wants to drown in blue sky.

What to make of myself, for I'm made of
stems and twigs and leaf-bits turning to rot,
my roots plunged deep beside a still water.

I don't worry too much as long as somewhere
a girl opening a notebook begins to sketch bare
trees holding aloft an afternoon's loss of light.

One can't predict a stream's downhill course, but
one can trail behind the stops and starts and see
a tracing out of something deep inside the earth.

A Voice Imagined as My Own

I can, with little effort, produce inside me
a voice imagined—maybe my own but just as
likely someone waiting on the barn door to close.

What does it mean, though, to seek so much
meaning, rarely satisfied, seldom comforted,
always older but still a child before elders?

Fate, destiny, one's lot in life, what-have-you,
is a funny thing—sometimes it finds us,
and other times we have to go search for it.

Well, I was bored one day, and that's how
I stumbled into who I am. Now I wake up
busy, falling farther and farther behind.

I might as easily have become a shepherd
humming a lullaby, alone with stars, one
seeming to brighten, then beginning to move.

A Voice We Might Share

Evenings I sit on my porch and wave at hay bales
in a neighbor's field. Laugh if you must, but I'm
an old man who's decided that anything is life.

I know a stretch of woods where a perfect holly tree
can't be explained. Neither can this awe I feel when
an owl lifts from the sycamore, riding the air I breathe.

So much has been made of the monarch's beauty
and rightly so. Such wings are unassailable, and we
spend many sleepless nights in dreamless cocoons.

Go back—revisit all those fragments written in youth
when you hid out in the church basement counting bricks
and hadn't yet heard Issa whispering his own subtractions.

We should ask those questions we've been holding
back, if only for the conversation we'll then share—
the one full of vowels and utterly without subtext.

Increasing Affection

He loves the words he searches for but cannot
find, and why not—the vowels are like water
spilling over stones gone faint with evening light.

From the eaves, some bird calls again and again,
increasing his affection for this time of day. All
he sees are the tips of its claws grip the gutter.

The shade of an oak has a lengthening silence.
A clothespin hangs limp, unmoved for seven years.
An investigation is underway, nearing its close.

What's been left out of the conversation speaks
loudest; if a mountain could kneel, a hermit, looking
up from an easel, might notice and then bow too.

There's always one more moment holding on beyond
the trees' gathering calm only a short walk away
from where something long ago begun continues on.

Jeff Hardin

Poor Listener

With all I do to guard a moment, nonetheless
it heals itself. A leafless oak means more light
caresses the crumbs the sparrows steal away.

Someone picking up a rifle finds it turned
into a mandolin or one of those childhood
willow limbs that fended off the wind.

I'm just repeating what wiser men have said,
varying the emphasis of a word or two. Behind
my forcefulness, there's mostly only beckoning.

Dickinson spoke reverie into my thoughts. I'm
now on these errands, though I doubt I'll return.
I've tasted the muscadine's clutch at the sun.

Maybe all I've done—filling up notebooks
and wandering around—is talk to myself, poor
listener, but wherever I went, I never returned.

A Certain Slowness of Speech

Such a long life yet so little time to stay up
through the night, awaiting that moment
the owl leaves its tree to alight along the eaves.

I'm certain even my slowness of speech,
though I wish to leave nothing out, amounts
to passing a hand through an ocean's wave.

A few friendships remain, each one a pardon,
but not one soul knows that place in the creek
where I stood, age nine, having survived my old life.

After two days of rain, the clover heads whiten
in the midday heat while I search through a book
for a thought I once had in response to a certain word.

So difficult to know an end is drawing near when
all I wish to do is follow how the wind suspends
the cedar limbs and then amends where it has been.

Assembling Many Voices

The contradictions in a single day are nothing
much to worry over. A moment's claim
may need rebuke to hear some grander reach.

A writer trusts that juxtaposing images are
deep in conversation and know some truth that
can't exist except to overhear their whisperings.

In God's ears, do all our prayers accrue as one?
Do some sound like rain on a roof, calming
the night, others like dirt tossed down on a grave?

Perhaps the mockingbird assembles all its voices
because to say a song across the storied lawn
is never wide enough to speak from every side.

We, too, require a congregation, voices stumbling
over each other, leaping forward, backward, just
to wring from ourselves a word worth this ache.

Point of View

When a voice comes to comfort, I mostly accept it,
but then other times reject it, good counsel or not.
I stare at the leaves and wonder what they think.

I can't keep up. I fall farther and farther behind.
In my defense, the script I've been given to speak
erases the words' magnificence before I can say them.

I remember now how I posed for Rodin. Where
re those sculptures, I ask, knowing full well
they were lousy—he smashed them to shards.

I thirst for the shine off a pearl in the moonlight.
What does *I thirst* mean? Well, for starters, I'm
standing by grapevines down the lengths of my youth.

My problem, as always, has been point of view.
I speak as myself; then I speak as the wind.
I speak as the forest floor and each twig that falls.

Jeff Hardin

Reaching in the Hive

A path through woods can point my direction,
but getting lost among vines and limbs reminds
me why I wake when no one else has stirred.

I'm not looking for martyrdom or my name
to be remembered—just a field of snow
cand my footprints borne away into the earth.

An old woman's weeping and prayers are not
to be mocked. I don't claim to know what wind
an oak steers elsewhere away from my house.

The real work's casting off what weighs me
down so I can stand inside a self that reaches
in a hive amid a swarm of warning voices.

Looking up sometimes, I see a radiant face: I am
hushed to hear my being heard by someone else—
was I speaking or praying? Was I even there?

27

Talking of Gratitude

Headed toward one thought, you'll meet another
and lose direction. Some trees grow beautiful
for bending all they are to touch the evening light.

In interviews, a man risks ridicule with his criticisms,
when maybe we should give some leeway and listen
in hopes that half of what he says could be the truth.

When the woman talked of gratitude, some people
in the audience dismissed her right away. Their
derision was the same as for murderers of children.

Friends writing letters across years can't seem
to get the phrasing right. They've yet to map
the path between the back steps and the barn.

He kept saying the subject was "you" and not
that tire swing left out beneath the oak all winter,
snow collecting, a bouquet offered up and melting.

The Music of Another Thought

Not once have I confused an ash tree for a statue
or a pile of creek stones for a basilica in Rome,
but daily I forget the trust inside a sparrow's song.

I admit I turn to poems to hear the music of another's
thoughts, to touch existence on the face, to lean
a little closer toward a thought that likewise bows.

That I stood in a shiver-down of sycamore leaves
while one leaf hid my face from passing traffic
is proof enough I do not need to come to much.

So many details I've forgotten or ignored, though
I look forward to the day when each is shown
to be the intercession my fallen life required.

Forgive me if I seem distracted—sometimes I am
deep inside a song deep inside the deepest self I am
farther down inside the inside that is all and only God.

Another Language

Jeff Hardin

A Word That Means How Each Moment Offers a Sermon

Here and now I stand in a Promised Land, though
I don't remember wandering, nor an old land's
poverties, nor anyone who might have followed me.

What is there to say about any gift given, especially
the ones unknown? The voice I think my own could
have moved to another as easily as leaves on a pond.

"And yet the books," Milosz says, and I've listened
for thirty years. I knelt right there in a library aisle
and studied his words like a monk holding scripture.

Each day, I've tried to begin a new life, sometimes
every hour. I lived half a day in a magnolia tree,
and so many selves abandoned me, fearing such joy.

It's hard to say which moment prayed the others
into being. Some stone tossed back to water might
have been a sermon lost from the History of Souls.

A Word That Means How Each Moment Is Both Vehicle and Tenor

Would you speak if every moment were a chess game
and all your words and pauses—attempts to reconsider—
were repositioned to confirm another's long-held views?

How to get back to a beginning absent anything but
how a few leaves borne on morning wind proclaims
how the loss of who one is may be all that will remain.

A dogwood growing at the base of a cedar, yet for
twenty years, I left it there. Years from now, I might
discern which was vehicle and which was tenor.

I live in the aftermath of Transtromer's "Schubertiana"
and add to his list of what must be trusted if I'm to go
on living when so much so easily could wipe me away.

For an hour, I stand inside meaning, as though it were
a sage grass field, all those stalks, like moments, one
into another, twining and flowing and following along.

A Word That Means What We Give Our Minds To

My father sketches out the boot heel of Missouri
and gives his mind to men and children bent to fields
they never straightened up from in all their years.

A hoot owl wakes me from this life I stumble through,
inviting anyone to join me. These words I trace confirm
I seek a way to stand inside a silence that erases me.

I love a song whose only word, repeated, is "rejoice."
All my favorite words are variations on this theme.
The soul I am can sense its rising from the ground.

So often, anything returned to is an absence weighed
against a self the self no longer is or cares to be.
A sparrow, steering skyward, stalls the present tense.

Like us, saplings metonym the selves they'll one day be.
All things manifest remind the mind to say *Amen*.
A slight wind bends again the reed lengths slendering.

A Word That Means the Silence Between One Word Joined to Another

Looking out over tops of trees, I grow disinterested
in anything but being a soul. Leaf stems trembling
and leaping about signal fall winds are drawing near.

And now the crows in a ruckus have reclaimed
the hillside. The truth I believe in needs no one,
least of all me, to defend it. I don't even say *Amen*.

Have I admitted how many times I mistook
Plato's words for my own? How likely the light
I claimed to witness was one more passing shadow.

My youth was formed by men and women standing
in sanctuaries, testifying and offering up prayers.
A furrow or grocery aisle is one more fellowship hall.

I could be wrong, but silence between one thought
joined to another holds the notes of hymns I sang
to which now, hummed low, I leap to add this one.

A Word That Means How I Have Lived a While Longer

In each of my joys, there's a grief at the core.
In each of my griefs, there's a gate before
a valley, my entering the only gift I can bring.

Lord, I begin, then break off into bird cheeps
and oak leaves scuttled over stones. Once
I was persimmons dropping into tall grass.

I wonder even now what prayer I've gone past,
how I might have stopped to live a while longer
with this or that rain-eye widening the pond.

The more I study my own heart, the less I'm
willing to say what happens when one person
opens a book and another attaches a wire.

I talk so much about kindness because I can't
discern what reveals itself between notes
when a song gets closer to the silence it holds.

A Word That Means How Theme Has Many Directions

I keep rediscovering things overlooked years ago.
Perhaps I'm not myself but, instead, someone
who stooped to move a fallen limb from the path.

Mercy as a theme has many directions, touches
rustlings in the thistle thickets and poems never read
and more than one word the widow keeps to herself.

The river I grew up next to meanders my thoughts,
these words I offer silt-stained and drug up from
the down-deep depths of a current drawn north.

In time, my lineage comes clear—I was birthed
each morning I sat on my porch and stared at
crepe myrtle limbs branching to branch again.

What else should I say but that I'm waiting
on a heaven that reddens the timelessness
of one moment not yet becoming another.

Jeff Hardin

A Word That Means the Fullness of a Moment's Prophecies

The prospect of saying one more thing about maples?
The mind in its poverties hasn't abandoned hope
just yet. It keeps speaking to avoid some final word.

Who thought comfort would be incessant? Who thought
the right poem would be stumbled upon, then taken in,
one more explanation of the holy, the unfathomable?

Last night's rain ticks down through October's leaves.
All these years, I've tried to find a new tense: an owl
on the roofline, a hay bale's stillness at the base of a hill.

No word for the word that is almost but not quite there
on the tongue. I see through a sliver, believing it the whole
scene. I'm walking among raindrops stalled upon the air.

Would that I could hold what is happening in the fullness
becoming this singular moment prophesying all around
me as the drenched-deep root of me drinks of the fill.

A Few Words Left Behind

I've no desire to use a different voice with you
than with a white oak sapling, moss I walk upon,
or creek stones. Even a falling leaf I take as confidante.

When bewilderment descends, I give up searching for
my hidden name, the one a willow flings into grass.
I turn back toward the fencerow, its six or seven posts.

Imagine a language pieced together from archaic words
we thought we left behind. I could spend all evening
staring at two trees at the far end of this snow-soaked field.

Our people, years ago, would plant an apple tree yards
from the house to draw the bugs away. A lesson is there
for those who wish to keep life's sweetnesses too near.

The cold's moved in to cancel what I've stored away.
Will I make the spring? It's envy I have—but also
love—for how the grasshopper gets to fling itself away.

Another Language

So long as someone's wandering a sage grass field,
we'll likely hear the music of that other language
passed back and forth between the river and the sky.

You won't catch me apologizing for piddling I did
as a child—even now I look down and can't explain
why no stick is in my hand to drag along behind me.

In the middle of the night, my father would wake us
to drive the backroads of a universe's silence. Now,
no one can convince me I don't belong to heaven.

Why aren't we asking each other for assurances?
I'll give you my voice, and you give me yours. We'll
let that be the start of prayers we'd never find alone.

As far as I can tell, the savior of this world wrote
only in dust the sins of those who stood nearby. We
can't know his handwriting except where we kneel.

Listening to Words

The words of Solomon have cursed us all with
listening toward the hope of a wisdom unknown.
Seventeen years between thoughts that might matter?

Then I hear Stevens and his evasions of *as*.
Maybe Jesus spoke words unrecorded when he
stood in their midst and quietened the storm.

Rilke's panther keeps studying the crowd.
A milkweed pod waits in a field each time
I walk past that line I was told not to cross.

What a child I must have been, already in love
with the next thousand years as I knelt toward
creek shallows, following my darting thoughts.

What I learned is likely just one part of a scene
framed by a window at the edge of a kingdom—
syllable, phoneme, stem on a leaf blowing past.

Jeff Hardin

A Word That Means Climbing Inside a Moment

Nothing in my hands again, having slipped back
into my old role of wondering what comes next
and why what I give gets brushed to the side.

Months without rain and now today a drizzle—
long overdue, a waste to the parched. Hummingbirds
steer through crepe myrtles without a damp wing.

Let's call this summer the one that should not have
happened. What of the fall to come? And the winter?
We'll be limping toward spring if we make it at all.

I admit I need more than the usual reminders. When
the bright world turns dull, I struggle through a prayer
whose words I can't taste, whose tone I can't hear.

I'll pack up what remains and climb inside a moment
no one knows exists, one barely humming to itself,
tucked back in a ledge above the falls, outside of time.

A Word That Means How Little Is Accounted For

Thinking of the moments just after Cain slew Abel.
Thinking of the blood, remittance for nothing.
Thinking if I'd been there, which face I would be.

Easy to think I know the next choice I'll make,
to wade into water or to skip a rock across it, but
this world proves only how little I've accounted for.

Late-changing leaves let loose in a lack of wind,
an easy biography, and spaces between barn walls
look out on eternity when I press my face close.

We'll scoff at a man climbing a ladder to touch
the moon? Then tell me why we linger with
the story of Narcissus bent toward his own face.

I guess I was told so often as a child to dump
the evening scraps out back, that now it's easy
to think so little of tossing out parts of myself.

Jeff Hardin

A Word That Means What Separates Us From Our Souls to Come

Though he was old, I wished another twenty years for
him to say his peace and blessings on the wrens, on how
the night descends to crowd in close and tuck him in.

It's not enough to know the afterlife is coming next.
I want, right now, to know the knowing I'll know then.
I want my wanting to be hollowed out and filled.

I'm reaching skyward on a night like this one
when wisteria has drenched the yard with scent,
a handbreadth separating me from my soul to come.

Must I always make sense, draw right angles,
keep track of the books on my study floor?
Following a feather, I'll still arrive somewhere.

What if these gifts I bring were never meant to be
discovered but, instead, stand behind my words
as something faint I'll never find my way to say?

A Word That Means the Joy of Being Wrong

I love those ridiculous ideas no one can prove.
I've made wild mistakes, but studying the reed's
sway at the pond's edge wasn't one of them.

One reason the poet sings "That's true, that's true"
is so he won't forget the joy of being wrong,
of being cast off like a stone from the path.

If you meet me on the street, don't be surprised
if offered sweet gum balls from my hand into yours.
We're two with consciousness, so gifts are all we have.

My daughter lying prostrate at the lily's stem
is reaching back in hunger to those books she read,
into phonemes that sturdy the clutch of her cells.

Go right ahead and tell stories of brave men.
I think I'll go on listening for small steps of
the mouse out there in the cucumber field all night.

A Word That Means How Little the Self Truly Wants

Not much is required to believe how little the self
truly wants—Bach says as much and Stafford near
dawn. A word, then quiet, then what's after that.

My thoughts turn to Issa—private moments he
must have endured, thinking on his children dead.
Two centuries afterward, I still pray for his grief.

There was an old man I knew who got more productive
with age, planting gardens, writing letters, wandering
through plum thickets, bucket in hand, gathering.

Without compass or chart, Dickinson was a slow
rower, still reaching more Edens than others her
century. She kept to herself how often she capsized.

I'm no longer interested in all I've acquired, petty
accomplishments, discarded hopes, reimagined pasts
and futures. I want to turn now toward all that I missed.

Toward an Answering Day

A Day Not Far From This One

What's this need to "say things right," as though
a voice had power to make words absolute. Only one
said, "It is finished." We say, "What comes next?"

We give speeches, write books, compose symphonies,
try to stand in the silence extending from our words,
but all the while, we're only salmon leaping upstream.

Grandmother's prayer journal goes up in a funnel.
Such loss is hard to take, but we knew her prayers
could not be bound, would fly out over the world.

Grandfathers, grandmothers, uncles, parents, everyone
on the porch, telling the same tales as always, yet
nothing seemed predictable, nothing already known.

A day not far from this one will also come and go.
From chestnut trees, extinct, leaves continue falling.
What I've whispered to night wakes shining from dew.

Believing Toward an Answering Day

Morning or evening, when I hear the dove call,
I don't mind being the orphan I am, though
I've never been far from the calling of home.

Across a hollow, some late light starts to burn.
I'll watch for a while and imagine a child studying
scenes that emerge from the tip of her brush.

What am I waiting on? the news of my life?
some patchwork truce to the back and forth
between light and shade on an autumn leaf?

So thin is the prayer of a man who complains.
I hope not to be him, though I fear that I am,
for my joy sometimes, too, is an open complaint.

When I hear the dove, I breathe who I am through
limbs toward the stars at the end of my breath. I
breathe my believing toward an answering day.

Jeff Hardin

As the Day Before, So the Day After

One song can sometimes last all day, not one
note decaying, just pure purpose and presence.
And then there was yesterday, its now-empty rooms.

Life's done with so many of us, gone on to visit
others. We sense how small our bodies really are.
No longer do we pitch ourselves from couch to floor.

As kids, we knew that climbing took us never far enough.
A part of us kept going and can't be summoned back. How
often, without knowing, have we been another's still-life?

For some, the future departs even before it gets here
—as though a page were missing, a key image or word,
and a life were meant to study what it moves along without.

As a child, a field nearby was world enough for me. A man
sneezing sent chickens toward the barn. Life was a leaning-
down fencepost, two or three nails too deep to get hold of.

A Kind of Day Anyone Could Have

I know too much sweetness envelops my thoughts.
I should get bedraggled or destitute. I should
give up these syllables for the gutturals of grief.

Echoes return, though I'm seldom certain of their
source. A lifetime of reading, and all I can say
is the words overlap and blur the whole thing.

Towns once passed I have imagined as home,
fitting myself to the sounds of their shops.
I shake out bread crumbs from letters I receive.

I confess: it wasn't my hand that cast the first
stone, but only because I was off to the side,
too busy amassing and arranging my pile.

Whatever's worth finishing is worth starting again.
A few wrong roads lead to years made of joy.
Beneath snowdrifts, some seeds are opening their eyes.

Jeff Hardin

The Problematic Nature of Time

Good thing I am no historian, for I'd rather trail
a broken stick through creekside leaves and waste
the afternoon than claim this date is crucial to our times.

Some hear the reach of time: it says "Perhaps." Others
conclude—through famine, prosperity—there is a plan.
But it's just you and I? Can I trust you're worried too?

Beware: you're being stolen for another's portrait of himself.
Beware: tomorrow rhymes with something in your past,
though many years will be required before it's clear just what.

Do I diminish or blaspheme to say a stone beside
a fallen tree reminds me—if I withhold my praise—
that everything I see is poised to step in for my slack?

I have my lasting questions, though I won't be sharing them.
I wake some nights: for hours I have helped a dead child's
mother hold a make-shift tent above his footprint in the yard.

That Pitcher on Vermeer's Table

Not much happens in the time frames I predict.
Off course by ten years or a lifetime, I can't tell.
I offer a clutch of zinnias, their brilliance withered.

Though not widely known, I've drunk for years
from that pitcher Vermeer placed near blue cloth.
Even with eyes closed, I'm conjugating light.

Two ironwood trees lean out from one another,
intimate for almost half a century. We'd never tell
their roots from one another, sewn above, sewn below.

Compliments come pouring in, but here's the truth:
the one who turns his pockets out may be a miser
full of indignation, a mouthpiece for his emptiness.

Why the purple tanager chased in fits and starts
the yellow butterfly, I'd be afraid to speculate,
though in my thoughts, I'm darting here and there.

Jeff Hardin

Since Possibility Is Aesthetically Higher Than Reality

If all a young boy wants to do is wander through the yard,
a sketchbook in his hands, let's let him take all day.
What shame or harm can come of his attentiveness?

Question or assertion—either way, words lined up
are metaphor for thoughts that can't be tempted
to remain, and we're careless caretakers anyway.

Poets keep insisting on a single moment, as though
its worth outweighs the others, as though we get just
one and not this long succession adding up to more.

It seems we think in opposites and extremes when
what consoles might be how dogwood limbs reach
around the nearest trunk and look like an embrace.

What kind of life creeps along not conscious of its end?
Let cool wind remind us May is near. Tell the truth:
is there a joy more lasting than a miles-long look at the sky?

An Answer Full of Questions

My thoughts on the subject of self come and go.
The feel of the sun on my face fills my cells.
I'm merely a guest inside everything I know.

The question I pose is how to start a sentence
with a silence full of questions grieved enough
to soothe this need I have for fuller answers.

Whatever it was I wanted for myself, I've now
forgotten. The next thought is never the next thought
since grace leaps forward and rewrites the plot.

Outside the gates, I hold these begging bowls,
poems above which people pause, looking in.
It's true my emptiness holds the width of the sky.

Ships set sail; planes find their runways; someone
stares down the hollowness of the last day he lives.
Another whispers blessings out ahead, and joy.

Having Tired of Recent Stories

Tumble on over, bag in the wind, right on out of my
yard. I might follow. And squirrel who can't stop
dancing on oak leaves, that's my kind of music too.

Last night I wept for the many who died this week.
I turned the coverage off and watched the ivy's green.
Worthless grief—what could I do? I knew no names.

Hawks chase each other down the driveway, veering
through overhanging limbs. I've read all the poets—
few catch that sound or swerve their lines as well.

We're here together for a while because we've seen
so much no one person can grasp or bear it all. We shield
each other so the light won't clutch us, turn us into dust.

After a giant wave, some loved ones—we know—will not
be seen again. "I still have hope," a stunned survivor says.
So quickly prayers begin to lift for her...and now this one...

A Few Grains Shifting

What were you thinking? that tomorrow finally
arrived? that we were standing somewhere other
than a graveside, fresh flowers already wilting?

There was that poem that shifted a few grains
in the silo, creating a pocket of air for the child
to breathe long enough his father could find him.

The neighbor's cows set the morning in motion.
The porch boards warp a little more each spring.
The intent of each purpose has yet to be known.

After an hour of reading, only a few words
remain—just as, walking the woods, you remember
a hollowed-out beech with bees spilling forth.

I, too, believe the things of this world have
messages to preach, for how could I not,
the air full of wind full of pollen and seeds.

Jeff Hardin

An Appraisal of the Situation

Someone steals the one good idea I have—
maybe a lifetime's work—but I get in line
when my turn comes and offer my admiration.

I'm seldom surprised by loss nor far from laughter.
A more useful idea would be to turn my efforts
toward understanding motives, especially my own.

Was there, in truth, such a thing as ownership?
I long ago gave up answers I found. I sought
to know a truth I couldn't hold or even believe.

An appraisal of the situation reveals at times
I stole from myself, one face stepping forward
while another, unnoticed, went quietly away.

These words too—the ones I found, the ones
I thought described my thoughts—stepped
forth because others were pushed to the side.

The Likelihood of Answers

Where's the praise song for conversations we're
blessed with never having to endure? No use
wasting words that waste the thoughts we are.

I'm not certain what I hold in my hands belongs
entirely to me. Maybe I escaped, and everything
I call my own was supposed to be another's share.

So many thinkers straining to find the shape eternity
casts on what we think we know reminds me of
a scarecrow trying to hold a field of beans intact.

Even with everything Pascal said, he was merely
a child standing at a blackboard, shifting his feet,
admiring most the answers he couldn't understand.

Maybe our hands are best made for breaking bread.
Rain falling turns dust to mud. How many miracles
of seeing lie waiting and trampled about our feet?

Jeff Hardin

The Work of the Centuries

If I sit for an hour and watch leaf stems tremble,
I'm doing the work of the centuries, my prayers
aware of how little the centuries have changed.

I tell myself the oak I pass daily remembers
my steps and waits for my approach. The shape
its limbs hold mirrors my hope to lift up the light.

Is it possible a child possesses a mind grown old
already? What else call his rollicking in leaf piles
or how he climbs to his feet with a radiant face?

One could do worse than be devoured, like Neruda,
by a lily breaking over water. I know I've been
stolen by the wake of a rowboat nudging the shore.

It's taken a while, but I've reached this conclusion:
I want only what the sparrow in the evening grass
wants, and the sparrow accepts whatever it finds.

Reminders of a Passing Hour

Sycamores overlooking the river tell the years,
though no one listens but the twigs trailing past
and the prayers of the leaves that can no longer lift.

One painting on a wall can calm a stormy night.
David, holding stones, needs only the one. A sky
full of snowflakes can't cover Thoreau's tracks.

An hour passing reminds me of how the hours
were full of fondness for how the feed barrel's
corn could heal itself after my hands dug deep.

If I thought I knew what the minds wants to know,
I'd be that scrap of paper in the fencerow, testing
the edge of the woods the map has yet to reach.

I hope all these guesses have mercy at their core.
If I haven't been gentle, then nothing's been true.
Though I never ate manna, I'm nourished the same.

Coming into an Inheritance

Jeff Hardin

Coming into an Inheritance

How many poems about visiting recluses
in search of wisdom have I read by now?
I should know more than this empty solitude.

Someone has her errands and the memory
of a cottonwood beneath which a whisper
fluttered up prayer-like into the leaves.

Moving along the creekbank's calm, I might
just come into an inheritance unknown by
those whose intimacies I treasure the most.

For a while, I knew only gratitude. I wandered
a back woods kingdom, letting go of how I used
to lie awake long past midnight's falling away.

Now where am I? Some page near the middle?
To whomever is listening, if you're reading aloud,
let's live in these vowels now softening our tongues.

Efforts to Graft One Logic to Another

The simplest exit appears, and you wonder where
it leads—beside which stranded face, along which
path, before or after the irrevocable turning point.

Faithfulness endures, or what passes for a kind
of attentiveness necessary not to fall asleep
despite exhaustion increasingly announcing itself.

These efforts to graft one logic to another have
stalled, but once an ideal has been imagined,
it shapes how to meet whatever then follows.

Suddenly the yard is full of leaves brushed along
by the sun's latest blossoming up the hillside.
Now what was it, once, that seemed so pressing?

Next month, bare branches will simplify the sky,
and most thoughts will turn inward to linger past
the moment the last moment seems to conclude.

Jeff Hardin

The Light Behind Forest Trees

My own expectations are a hindrance—that's clear.
Whether happiness or grief or a mixture of both,
what happens will happen and none of it be error.

Now I remember standing creekside and looking
upwind. The light behind forest trees revealed
back behind this world another world peering in.

When someone claims she cannot follow words
another speaks clearly, in tenderness, I understand
she was never on the side of meaning anyway.

Let's put down books for a while and just sit
in the middle of the beings we are—threadbare,
vagrant—vapors caught up on a shimmer of breath.

Anymore, I've given up wanting to know what
anyone would have me know or believe. I want
only to taste what the butterfly swerving believes.

Risking Ridicule

There weren't poems enough about woodpiles when
we had them, and now our minds won't be given to
contemplation of the cold, the work that still remains.

I watch robins in the grass, an hour of sprints, beaks
plunged once, twice. If only painters were assembled,
composers, choreographers, pastors, philosophers...

I know I'm risking ridicule, but I have to say I love
how from the highest limb, a bird's faint song feels
as all-surrounding close as any whisper in my ear.

No need to rush me—all my life I've walked around
a pond at the edge of memory, empty-handed but
rich in spirit. I'm grasping cattails, reeds, the wind.

Whatever happens—thought, gesture, screen door
closing—brings me to the edge of choice, though
even countless choices may not set one soul aright.

Sunlight Back Behind the Clouds

A few drops of rain this evening, hardly enough
to wet the tongue, and that purple bird goes
skimming past again in a shining all its own.

When the air is weighed down with the scent
of magnolia, and the morning has yet to begin,
I lean toward holiness a little more than usual.

The little I grasp I reach for with both hands.
A next thought may sharpen the edges of clouds.
If only one breath could halt the earth's spin.

I've been wrong before and often enough
that I've come to accept my odious failings,
comforted by listening to leaves letting loose.

Isn't sunlight back behind clouds a reminder
to wait? Am I not weightless with the smallest
of joys? Even my yes is lifting, is fluttering away.

Wrens Hopping Up the Dogwood Limbs

I'm sure today had other plans, but I'm still here.
Between me and the cattails, a race: who'll grow
taller? Who looks more ridiculous leaning in wind?

Come fall, I'll set up residence at the windowsill
and be an old man for a season. Just me and oblivion
and afternoon naps where I'm a poem of a single word.

Given a chance, what would I do? Yes, what *would* I do?
I'd stretch out in the creek and be a stone gone smooth.
I'd climb up the spider's web to catch the morning light.

Distraction. Distraction. It's all distraction. Except
when wrens start hopping up the dogwood limbs.
They're dancing, I know, so why not join their call?

Imagine narcissus bulbs one day growing into stalks
of corn. What would a nation be then—late in a barren
world—if self-love turned into listening toward others?

Jeff Hardin

A Fire We Might Touch

New growth on the tulip tree is currently seventeen
sprouts. Next week, who can say? I wonder what
reachings toward my life some later season brings.

Lucky for me, the grammar of rainfall makes sense.
Sometimes, two days of reading, other times three.
I can move through the centuries in an afternoon.

The little I grasp I reach for with both hands.
A next thought may sharpen the edges of clouds.
If only one breath could halt the earth's spin.

Though outshined by dew, I feel no disappointment.
There's so little time to be the silence of barn hay.
I'll take what light I find wherever it stalls the dark.

Messages keep arriving, though I'm not to be trusted
—some are obvious and others opaque.
A yard full of twigs speaks the wealth of the stars.

Of one who believes such claims, I hear the sneers,
dismissals, rumblings, and gripes. I've tried not
to calm one ember of the fires we've yet to touch.

Coming into an Inheritance

Passing Untended Fencerows

So many elders keep their minds—as lucid
as ever—astute observers whose insights
make our concerns look foolish and trite.

I try my best not to trade upon the sufferings
of others, but it seems these days even to breathe
comes at the expense of someone overlooked.

Am I wrong to nod agreement when I pass
untended fencerows, redbud and sassafras
beginning a processional the wrens follow?

I can't help but praise a world where one man
enjoys a lifelong conversation with Vermeer's
verdigris while another listens toward coyote yelps.

Imagine narcissus bulbs one day growing into stalks
of corn. What would a nation be then—late in a barren
world—if self-love turned into listening toward others?

Though unsure how old I really am, I've come
to believe the eyes of anyone stopping to look
inside mine, afloat on this weeping I failingly hide.

Jeff Hardin

Nudges, Reminders, Fields, Songs

My insistences are mostly nudges, reminders.
What's a field without ponds, one at least,
a wrinkled face saying, "Look at the sky."

The woodpile is shrinking and has been for years.
I'm speaking, of course, of the fire in the voice,
our words now ashes we stare at between us.

Black perch—what a message!—rode the current,
not the eddies, not under some fallen log. I had
to walk out toward them to coax them to shore.

The timbers of the barn on my Papaw's place
must have framed up my sense of the universe.
Some satisfied lowing comes down from the fields.

Two pews ahead—I remember now—a widow
sang loudly, always off key. The congregation
nestled her voice, making a way for her praise.

Reaching Toward the Center

Remember those men who whittled and swapped
stories on storefront pews before the realness of
their lives was changed to myth, used against them?

The kids in the side yard made a kingdom of the oaks
and wrote no laws upon roots or the dirt. Vowels were
full of haplessness and blue through branching limbs.

If we could talk to one another—without reservation—
I think we'd use no words at all. We'd sit and weep
at how another's presence amplifies the air we breathe.

I don't want much besides this deepening anonymity
and a trail that gets closer to the center of my life.
I want a moment before death to sing a song of praise.

In the county of my youth, I touch the graves of all
my names. I place a hickory nut squarely on the creek
winding the county's length. My thinking climbs inside.

Jeff Hardin

Abundance

One taste of a peach and I'm on that farm again,
a lost child high in a tree, sunlight on my tongue.
Who needs a passport or a schedule to keep?

What would Heraclitus do at the edge of the sea?
How far should one wander from wandering itself?
At the end of each poem, another poem begins.

To sign my name like the hummingbird does.
To quieten my voice like the moss and weeds.
To think like the butterfly sketching on air.

I've been called a nutcase, a dimwit, and worse
by those who never sat beneath the ivy's breath
or allowed an hour's radiance to unspool its leaves.

Daily, I try to fathom abundance I don't deserve.
My mind is too small but fathomless too. I have
only these words being born and the spaces between.

Seconds in Several Branches

The cardinal lives seconds in several branches,
then drops down into grass to strut around. Even
Derrida concedes its red cannot be cancelled out.

A lot could be resolved if I listened for steps
of monks along far-up paths a mountain hides.
The rain comes to wash away the evening rain.

A weakness, I know, but I never tire of thinking
of how little my talent, yet how large my joy,
whether I sit or walk or sing among furrows.

I won't dispute I lack the discipline to praise
whatever burdens I'm to bear, yet haven't I
proved I'm like forsythia flailing inside a storm?

Nothing wrong with lingering, if what I hear are
falling plums or three terse wing strokes of a heron
rising up to leave me here, becoming elsewhere.

Rule of Thumb

It takes one hypothetical to open a gate leading
to fields hidden from view. Despite quiet stanzas,
Stafford's voice could redirect a river's course.

Should apologies be witnessed by the morning
star? Shouldn't blueberries be involved? It's
clear we don't know which next steps to take.

The difference between my errors and successes
is negligible, and anyway, what business do I have
trying to track waves gone forth from my rowboat?

Friend or foe, I advise not listening to these rants
if you think a man silly for bowing down to sip
from spring water while speaking to his thirst.

Parting company, some friends know they won't see
each other again, not in this life. What issues from
a word takes centuries to form our mouths around.

Benediction

In this stand of pines, I've chosen rain. So much
else I might have claimed—bitterness, regret—
instead, five minutes, ten, this brilliance of time.

A life makes a pattern seldom seen, even if we're
the one living it. What does it matter, though? One
day trees are leafless, another day heavy with fruit.

This image of being lost in woods then finding
an open space to lie down in—is this a memory
or one more necessary but useless metaphor?

Not that a decision must be made or conclusion
reached, but that a kindness might settle upon
a nation, as a hand might touch stalks of sage.

A hundred-year-old man wants one more trip
to the falls. As he has done so many times before,
he doesn't wipe the mist descending to find his face.

Jeff Hardin

Point of Origin

In the coolness after rain passes through, the sky
to the west is a shade of purple never seen before.
So what if I exaggerate—I do so out of reckless awe.

From the first note, the harp lives in denouement.
One's life lived before seems only rising action.
A flute makes an interlude between two breaths.

My own point of origin involved a wheelbarrow
full of rocks wheeled out past the barn's bent shadow.
Sometimes, though, I knelt where a doe had stood.

Home from school, I followed Papaw from woodshed
to hog-trough to feed barrel to woods trail. Evenings
on the porch, we sat barefooted and sang to the stars.

I figure whatever fortune I had was as much as I could
bear. I lay on pine needles; I sampled wild plums; cast
here and there, I held on tight to the bones of the wind.

83

Acknowledgements

Some of these poems appeared in the chapbook *Generosity for a Later Generation* (Seven Kitchens Press, 2020).

Gratitude to the following journals in which the following poems appeared:

2River	"A Few Grains Shifting"
	"A Kind of Day Anyone Could Have"
Bracken	"A Few Words Left Behind"
Connotation Press	"The Problematic Nature of Time"
	"That Pitcher on Vermeer's Table"
	"Since Possibility Is Aesthetically Higher Than Reality"
Delta Poetry Review	"Poor Listener"
	"A Word That Means What Separates Us from Our Souls to Come"
The Grindstone	"Morning Light along Sage Grass"
Heartwood Literary Magazine	"A Voice Imagined As My Own"
Louisville Review	"A Day Not Far from This One"
New Madrid	"Abundance"
	"Generosity for a Later Generation"
	"What We Give Our Minds To"
North American Review	"Listening to Words"
Peacock Journal	"Coming into an Inheritance"
	"A Fire We Might Touch"
	"Sunlight Back Behind the Clouds"
	"Having Tired of Recent Stories"
	"An Answer Full of Questions"
Poetry Northwest	"Studying the Sages"
Potomac Review	"As the Day Before So the Day After"
Stirring: A Literary Collection	"Believing toward an Answering Day"
Sublunary Review	"Wrens Hopping up the Dogwood Limbs"
	"The Work of the Centuries"
Sugar House Review	"A Word That Means the Joy of Being Wrong"
Quiddity	"A Certain Slowness of Speech"

About the Author

Jeff Hardin is the author of seven previous collections of poetry: *Fall Sanctuary* (Nicholas Roerich Prize); *Restoring the Narrative* (Donald Justice Prize); and *No Other Kind of World* (X. J. Kennedy Prize), among others. *The Hudson Review, The Southern Review, Image, Swing, Bennington Review, The Laurel Review,* and *Southern Poetry Review,* among others, have published his poems. An eighth-generation descendant of the founder of Hardin County (Savannah, TN), he has taught for more than 30 years at Columbia State Community College in Columbia, TN.

Visit his website: **www.jeffhardin.weebly.com**.

Similar April Gloaming Titles

All Things Holy and Heathen
Chelsea C. Jackson

Dear Excavator
Evan D. Williams

The World Black, Beautfiul, and Beast
C.I. Aki

Love Letters from an Arsonist
David van den Berg

What Haunts Me
Bernadette Geyer

The Wolf Can Smell This is My Acre
Klyd Watkins

APRIL GLOAMING

View our full catalogue at aprilgloaming.com